Jesus Te
How to be Happy

Sinclair Ferguson

This series looks at the teachings of Jesus. Read the story and discuss the pictures.

Illustrated by Jeff Anderson

Published by Christian Focus Publications, Geanies House, Fearn, Tain, Ross-shire, IV20 1TW, Scotland.

www.christianfocus.com Printed in the United Kingdom

Everybody wants to be happy. But lots of people don't know how to be happy.

We can be happy only when our lives are working the way God wants them to work. Otherwise things go wrong.

Jesus' way to be happy is to know that you are poor inside because of your sins. Only he can give you what you really need.

Jesus shows us that being his disciples brings us true happiness. His happiness is real, and it lasts for ever.

One day Jesus gathered all his disciples around him. He had already told them about his kingdom. He was to be The Great King.

Now he was going to teach them some very important things about how to live in his kingdom. Jesus sat down and began to teach.

‘First of all’ said Jesus, ‘I want to tell you about the happiness God wants you all to have. It is different from what most people think. So listen carefully.’

Here's what Jesus went on to say. Most people think that the best way to become happy is to get plenty of money. But there are very rich people who are very sad.

Most people think that the way to be happy is to avoid anything that makes you feel sad. Jesus' way is different. You can be happy only when you first become sad!

If you are sad about your sinful heart and ask for forgiveness, God will forgive all your sins for Jesus' sake. Then you can be really happy.

Most people think that the way to be happy is to be strong and always to be first.

Jesus says the way to be truly happy is different. The only happiness that lasts is letting Jesus do whatever he wants with your life.

Most people think that the way to be happy is by having everything you could ever want.

Jesus says that the way to be happy is by asking God to put right all the wrong things in your life.

Most people think that the way to be happy is to look after yourself first. ‘Look out for Number One’ they say.

Jesus says that we can be really happy only when we care for people who are poor and needy and people who have nobody else to help them.

Most people think that to be happy you must get what you want. Magazines have adverts for cars, houses and lots of other things that people want to buy. Jesus says you can have all these things and still not be happy.

The only thing that can make you happy is having a heart full of love for Jesus himself.

Most people think that the way to be happy is by making sure nobody gets in your way.

Jesus says that happiness comes to people who want others to know God's peace.

Most people think they could never be happy if they became disciples of Jesus. They think that if people said or did bad things to you because you belonged to Jesus you would be sad.

Jesus says that he has a special happiness to give to his disciples whenever they are alone or in trouble for his sake.

Jesus said, 'What good will it be if you gain the whole world, yet lose your soul?' Matthew 16: 26.

Are you truly happy? Do you love Jesus most of all? You can find Jesus' teaching about this in Matthew 5:1-11.